# The Last Island

Poems
By Mimi White

DEERBROOK EDITIONS
2008

PUBLISHED BY
Deerbrook Editions
P.O. Box 542
Cumberland, Maine 04021
207-829-5038

FIRST EDITION

ISBN 10: 0-9712488-8-5
ISBN 13: 978-0-9712488-8-5

On the cover:
Grape Leaves with Lesser Goldfinch Nest by Sharon Beals
with permission
Copyright © 2008 by Sharon Beals
www.sharonbeals.com

Cover and book design by Jeffrey Haste

# Contents

## I

## II

# III

for Rachel and Abby

in memory of Dorothy Ruth Kovitz Novack
(1915-1982)

*What makes the engine go?*
*Desire, desire, desire.*


from *Touch Me*—Stanley Kunitz

I

*There is always water*
*The sea moves beneath my feet*
*Like so many birds*

## She Watches a House Burn As If It Were Her Own

Love never ends the way we think.
It's no more imaginable
than the way we will die.
Over soup, chunks of potatoes,
he says, "I've been sad."
The soup is not thick enough,
his face is not his face.

He does not shave for days and tells her,
"I would have driven both of us
into a tree if I had known."
She tests a potato,
hard as a rock.

He pulls away from her slowly,
although he cannot get enough of her;
her scent is on everything.
When they make love
he brings her to the edge.
She craves the ebb, his tongue
that overpowers.
Then the rush. Not the release.
Not to be free from desire.

She watches a house burn.
This is the loss of language.
She cannot name what was hers:
a cotton dress, a mirror, a comb.

## Nightfall, Rodin Gardens

I remember the gardens in early December,
the empty chairs devoted to the body.

Leaves flew at me yet I did nothing
to save them.  One hand pulled at my collar,

the other stroked the lovers in their brutal postures,
groin and groin. Standing, twisting shoulders

exposed, brightly polished stone dying.
I crawled past the statues, knees aching,

palms embedded with glass,
into the bronzed arbor and burned in the wind.

I could not forget the grass, the smallest fragment
of our history. The green before and during.

How do I drag my body through a life or lie down
next to it, blindfolded, hands tied back?

The walls turned black, the crevices gray,
yet the Paris sky refused the night. *Aubergine.* Alive.

## Still Life Minus You

You sleep on a different rim,
　one that cracks
　　without reason like ice

that opens.
　I cannot see your limbs turn
　　in the blue undertow,

your colors fuchsia,
　magenta,
　　and that undulating

aquamarine. The landscape shifts,
　incinerates into dusk,
　　and heat rises in the fields

where lovers are paper
　silhouettes and they burn
　　like grass in a hot wind.

You walk in the sun,
　and here a shadow floats on snow,
　　an illusion

of how things are. Your voice carries
　distance, like a stitch,
　　and a button

slips into place.
  Over a chilly surface
    hibiscus climb, and birds

escape into the sky.
  I walk inside and freeze things
    the way they are:

A sprig tea set, the cups
  with the crooked handles,
    the painted, scissored leaves.

## Pleasures of the Natural World

When you were in The Canyon I read your guides
for the most dangerous routes:

plateau crossings, footholds in the sky, fingers closing
on air, heat pressing the body into dust.

When the woman sitting beside me opened her blouse
I wanted her breasts as an offering of my love for you

seeking pleasures of the natural world.
I could have touched her,

sunlight brightening her white blouse,
her nipples rosy as finger tips.

Tongue-tied, I wanted to be intentional, wanton
as the sun that meant nothing to her, as did the men,

pausing, passing, kicking stones,
waiting for the wind to feather her skin.

She was not beautiful, but dangerous with ease.
That's what you had said of me. I seemed at ease

with you and the light in the room. I wanted
their eyes on me. Consider this my weakest season.

The sea remembers salt & blood & shame,
while the mind floats above the head.

## The Crossing

A ferry carries me past
the last island, its edges
under water. Topside

I take the wind. Someone
tosses a queen, shuffles
the deck and the cards fly

into the sea. I am watching
the lovers rush the sun. He's
kissing her mouth. His hands

search places: *there*
*and there.* I stood in that blind spot,
reeling. The sky electric,

sudden flash of blue. Winter
buries memory yet I see
lizards, white stones before

you slipped from view.
We go away and then we
return means everything

when you have been
crushed by the heat.
He's crazy for her.

You can see it
in his hands
lifting the sheen

of her hair. Wrists
glaze her neck,
her faithless throat.

## The Moon is White

He wanted to undo something. Her hair.
Close the cupboard.  Cross the floorboards in light.

He moved like young men in her novel.
Late nineteenth century, their bodies

dry, calm leaves. Over the island
the sky was years away.

She studied his palm: an open box,
opalescent pearls, blue flames.

Ah, the thumb print on her nipple.
He balances the moon on his tongue.

## Shattered Branches

The limb was rotten and took the sky.
What small gesture was left dangling?

What sounds did you catch
of the stunned birds, their muted weather?

A sharp *crack* revises sorrow
into fractured moments: shattered branches

litter the earth and you look the same.
Earlier we had passed a car upside down

and smashed on the road's steep shoulder.
I had wanted to say something

that would bring us to the kitchen,
peaches in a glazed bowl,

you entering the room from mowing
or returning from a trail dangerous with shale,

but the car hung, suspended,
you falling back to me.

## Field Notes

I watched a bird
Flitting upside down
On a gray sky.

She was small as a thumb,
Striped with rust
And speckled rose.

I had thought to name her,
To locate her genus
In a color-plated guide.

The bird was neither
A robin nor a thrush,
But what stills my mind

Is what I know:
A pocket of feathers,
An assemblage of song,

And when there is no love
Left to extinguish,
The sky.

## The Lost Day

I remembered hearing the call of the kingfisher, his favorite bird. I meant to tell him to look at the sky, but I was distracted by the perfect weather, and by then the lost day came back to me:

She was young, lovely, and with a smile she knew how to hold. *Oh you came*—the delight in his voice. She stepped closer then. They talked easily, excitedly, with gestures that were reminiscent of time—theirs, ours. If the floor had not been moving. If I had not been caught between them, between her face and his. I could feel their heat, the purpose of another's body. I heard myself say something about home, where we lived. And where did she live? I had hoped to tame her, to make the day mine, but already the words trailed off toward the wrong story.

Later, in that same crowded room, and still later in our room, he and I would call it love. But it was not love. It was happiness. And such happiness.

The gift of being alive, and he held it out to her.

## Aubade

*At The Frost Place*

Rain has little to do
with love, yet
here you are.

All the trails up the mountain
are steep, you'd said,
thinking out loud.

Each has a scramble,
a rock face,
and in rain
could be dangerous,
you'd said, when I left
and drove north.

After last night's moon,
after the sharp
pencil line of mountain peaks
against dusk's falling
and rising sky,

rain spattering the screen
surprises, and my mind
races to locate
what bed is this
I wake in
without you?

## November's White Apples

Notice how the gold leaves spin
and the sky opens its black branches.

If I could hold November's
extravagant loss
that ushers forth
the earth's white meadows
I could arrive at the nexus
of ardor and faith.

Not long ago
one of us would have thought
the weather had changed
and brushed up our collars.

We walk a path
crusted with ice,
the air indivisible
from wind and shadow,
snow extinguishing
the sparrow's brief song.

We turn into it.
A fine dust flecks our faces,
the apples disappear.

## The Bells of Autumn

I entered late autumn
To receive the last note
You offered as praise.

My body climbed
One gold rung at a time
And the bells rang.

I witnessed the lilacs
Stalled in ice,
Knocking against the cold.

When I glanced back
I missed the place
Where the seeds had settled.

How unlikely
Wind could damage faith,
How unlikely winter's benediction.

## Looking for Luck

We crossed in a ferry with tiny windows
like slits into parts of dreams

and rolled from side to side and lost the sun.
A girl reading a book brought her face closer to the page

and her hair hid where she had gone.
This is how the islanders disappear

and return, one sewing, one singing,
one rehearsing the violin, her fingers pressing air.

Show me your losses and I'll show you mine, we say,
trading our share of misery like playing cards.

You counted twenty raptors and stopped
astonished at your own good fortune,

a white crown and golden talons on every other tree,
their wings and the beauty of the wind

turning your heart. I held fast to the thin edge of desire,
to forget must be like birds

forgetting the sky. I wanted to touch your sleeve,
a part of you that would not give way.

II

## Blue

All day I watch the pups
nip at each other's ears and roll
over each other's gray bodies.
Is the one who circles the shrubs
and barks at night the mother?
Is that the father
taking off through the field?

Oh everything is damp
and I grow strange
kneeling by my house.
As I wait for the fox to emerge,
the night brings animals
for me to smell:
A white dog walking the moon,
a badger, a family of mice
eating sugar cubes in a queer, yellow light.
I bury my face in the wolf's ruff
and sniff the house and the residue
of wind.  When I awake
the rhododendron's shadows
chisel an umbrella of black leaves
into the muddy earth.

*Come here. Come here, quick.*
Such pale wild eyes of blue.

## Snow in Autumn

A dog barking stole our sleep.
We watched the farmhouse windows
lose the shapes of trees.

A deer leapt white on white
then turned to the blackened hills,
while the stars rolled down the river.

I waited for the floor to creak,
for the wind to bring more rain.
The storm came and left as snow.

The rhythm of your breath
darkened my shoulder,
not your mouth on my skin.

O, the moon's halo, the brevity
of the earth's curve,
and you.

## Indigo Bunting

She pecks for insects, seeds,
bits of old grass.
The female of the species,
brown with variations, the land
darker where she flies,
the shadow of her passing
body a loose stitch
to mark a spot,
then vanish.

## Who Count the Dead

Red feathers disturb the snow's equilibrium.
Before and after revelation,

the dark world slumbers. A loss of reason
tilts the crimson sphere

yet the bud slips from its yellow socket
and we drink tea in a golden window.

Assume nothing: illness, safety, spring,
and begin with wonder—an unspeakable

subject, the coupling of the strange
with the divine: hailstorm/minute, beehive/prairie,

the dead and the living who count the dead
and finger the pleats in their pant legs.

Who drapes the coffins?
Who sleeps with one eye open

and eats the fiery sky?
Tomorrow, we'll rake spring rubble,

gather stones split by ice
and watch for the bluebird,

his rosy apron as he flies
remarkable and true.

## My Mother's Bureau

*The drawers slide to a close*
*and the brass pull rings.*

My hair brushes my shoulders
and my long arms make windmills.

My mother is in the kitchen
stacking milk-glass bowls

into the maple cupboards.
They clink like cowbells,

each sound
a pebble sinking in a river.

They slip past light
to the water's bottom.

I wish my mother would turn
her face toward mine.  I'd like

one word to carry
to the room's silence,

her voice from another place
far away from mine.

Her back the landscape
I sing myself to sleep in.

## An Apology for Silence

1. *Molly*

I've entered the kingdom of azaleas,
rhododendron ten feel tall.  A park,

a peaceful park.  No children, dogs, balloonmen
allowed. Rain falls and washes the earth.

Women, a line of summer dresses drying,
stand closest to the open grave.

In beautiful letters, from back to front,
we receive the sacrament

of sorrow, voices full black vowels.
A man leads my arm, my body

up the gentle slope.  My shoes fill
in the first few steps.  The land, its motion

surprises, as I rise above
my grandmother's grave.

2. *Dorothy*

When they lowered my mother into the ground
winter darkness heaved

pure white, crystalline blankness.
Small plastic letters announced her name,

spelled it out, as if we did not know
though cold speaks closer.

Yarmulkes fluttered and fell
and the Rabbi read with one hand covering his hair.

And while I had wished it so,
my mother did not rise or speak or lay

her hands open inviting me in.

## A Simple Love Story

In the story of the wolf, the sheep, the shepherd
silence is a terrible thing.
So what if he called that lie
into the domed sky,
clouds scudding across,
the sun lighting the leaves,
a single syllable called over
the river that darkened the grass
near the little village homes.
We all lie to find out who loves us.

They came running.
·He was happy to see
his father, his mother, his papa
hobbling up the hill,
aprons still tied, sleeves rolled
from bread-making,
boots caked with clay.
At night, asleep and content
on a bed sweeter than lilies,
so deep into his dreams he smiled

all through the slaughter.
The blood soiled the white,
the damp smell of loss rose,
the sky came down

and covered all he knew.
The bones, shaped like c's and l's,
spelled out no words
that could make things right.
"Wolf!" "Help!" meant nothing.

Down below they were distracted,
humming a bit,
starting a new day.
The sun already on the steep roofs.
steam rising off the cruel grass.

## HAARESCHNEIDERAUM: The Haircutting Room

They preferred women's hair to the hair
of men and children; it tended to be longer, thicker.

They preferred individual elegant waves,
finger curls, knotted locks.

They preferred the coarser strands of older women,
not grandmothers, but women whose children
were almost grown.

They preferred clean hair, hair with a sheen,
but that proved impossible.

They preferred the plaited to the smooth,
not for thread or mattresses, but to touch
as the plaits became unwoven in their official hands.

They preferred that the hair be brushed or combed,
but they collected all of it, even the tufts
pulled out in clumps.

They preferred ashes to bone and prized hair for stuffing
and stiffeners and felt hats.

They preferred what was useful, the tensile quality
of hair that proved essential
to the making of delayed action bombs.

They preferred industry;
at twenty pfennig per kilogram
the hair fetched a fair price.

They preferred to think of hair
in terms of bales.

They preferred harvesting to killing,
the hair first.

They preferred shearing the corpses,
no bleating, no one home,
the hair last.

They preferred the shape of the skull, the small
indentation at the nape of the neck.

They preferred lockets, snippets, keepsakes pressed
like roses in volumes of poetry.

## That Sheep May Safely Graze

*County Antrim, Northern Ireland, Good Friday 1998*

Last spring I saw a sheep go down
and knew she must be quickly turned
before the crows pecked out the eyes
and ripped her sides with bloody claws.
The farmer found her sight was gone,
but felt a pulse beneath the flesh.
He cut right there and lifted out
the mewing twins then left with them,
the hills turned black with night.
Beside Red Bay at Cushendall
the stench of rot filmed the air
and turned curachs and surf to gray:
now one more dead at the edge of land.
What brought me to this quiet coast
where glens turn green inside the sky
then plunge to sandy shore? I turned my head
to face the row of blackened roofs,
to watch the smoke of each banked flame
drift to meet the rains, then I drove North
and found the last who'd left her flock.
I think she lay where she was struck,
where wind or stream had stopped.
The rocks that bound the farmer's land
fell open like a sluice, and there they roamed
as if the green was theirs, the lane was home.
Still as air inside a hole, I grew accustomed
to the chill. The death of sheep became a tune

that ran above the farms and sea and settled
on the grass. In light that slants and leaves the hills
the sheep that stood were dried with mud.
They far out-weighed the ones who'd died.
They filled the fields with bleats and hoofs.

## Minus Zero

*Nothing to touch*
*except old paper*
*and two people talking.*

Since it is spring and red buds
disguise what one might be thinking,
just the other day

harbor light took me elsewhere
and to boats. Strange how the mind
is supple and bones

are singularly fixed in time.
On our morning walks,
my dog and I sniff for winter.

Even the matted chill
under old leaves
nudges him along,

deeper into the past,
and I check the wind
for a late March storm.

Let's go backwards,
he says, looking up at me,
as if he knew

that tides pull
the deepest channels
clean and

a dazzling moon
will lull me further
from *you* and *you* and *you*

whom I will forget
in the frenzy
of the garden's splendor.

I am ripping dead vines.
I am checking for damage.
And, if the bluebird

decides against all odds
to make my field her home,
I will still weep.

Next fall, next spring,
even in the zero hours of winter,
you will be song.

    *for Robert Creeley*

## The Singed Horizon

The world is lost to me,
my heart's wild fist
tossed with leaves.
I want to be in love,
but who can stand on that glossy island?

I walk the road that turns
toward the yellow marsh,
cold with the moon's phases.
As the sun escapes the singed horizon,
I assume light's salvation,
but beauty finds no place here.

The dog chases something lively,
inside the morning's arbor,
turns the soft earth
and pulls me through the thicket.
He sniffs each pile of dead leaves,
the edge of the forest, and underneath—
dank, and sweet.

## Your Dreams

At last I am not in them.
Perhaps I live in the small house
that's just out of view. How like me
to place myself at the edge
of your private darkness.
Today, the lake is more mystery
than repose.  I am willing the newest loon
into the cove, her smoky feathers and dark cap
starting to resemble her elders.
*I was born to tend your grave,*
I was going to write,
but then a twig brushed my shoulder
and you approached. Shyness,
like a paper soldier,
stands between us, shifting yet firm.
I am no longer beside you,
at the center of your dream's fluid armor.
Perhaps God is looking through this poem's
blue shell knowing we have more to say.
Dear One, what's yours is not mine.
I am the speck on the hill.
Waving.  Waving. Hello, *grass burning,*
*small plane touching down.* Goodbye.

## Sweet Girl

Leaves fill the sky outside your window
and remind me of the color of a bird
I once held in my hand.

A mother and daughter, we walk arm in arm.
Our chatter escapes into the shrubbery.
The hills rise and fall.

I thought this was the last best day
my sudden words spoken,
our heads inclined and touching.

Our voices tumble down the street, but we don't care.
The houses we pass are so big
pianos could slip right into their open windows

fill the white rooms with music.

*for Abby*

## What's Given

If you could see the swallows,
if you could sleep
in this house of light,
you would know that sadness
carries solitude
in its bony beak.
Harsh as it is, what's given
is also a clearing
in the forest. I cannot go there
with you. I am journeying
toward a golden bowl,
a leafless and stubborn
light. While you have the refuge
of heavy branches,
while your path is needled
green, find the opening.
I sense the turkey vultures
brooding, and I feel
the heat of a millennia of stones.
We do not choose
between suffering and life.
Remember the child
who pushed the witch
through the fiery door?
She was her brother's keeper.
And the stones blazed white.

*for Rachel*

III

## After Careful Consideration

Tonight I am going to study the moon.
I meant to last night, but was lulled
by the dark, the lake revising itself
into silence and song, water on stone.
I lay on the dock that tilts
with the weight of the body
and watched a plane dot on and off,
then bank toward Labrador,
island of snow and wind
and the most hospitable
people on earth.
I dreamed of a village
where we lived out our lives,
where you studied your knots and boats,
bent over a table late into the night.
I called to you, thinking you would hurt your eyes
working so long in the oil lamp's glow,
but I was wrong.
I was wrong about so many things.

## From The Isle of Bliss

This mossy solitude reminds me of you. Yesterday, I

watched a fox brush her tail against a blistered sun. It was as

if she had built a gilded temple, tucked and lit against the sky.

When I walk the streets, I unlearn the path back to

the city's crumbled arches. My feet remember a wilder

passage, a distant hill.

At night, when incense smudges the island's ancient

orchards, I wait for your words to reach my lips.

## Night Blooming: Two Tellings

Do you think you have a heart, can you tell?

Then show me where to touch it with my heat.

I dreamed a lover tapped it with a tool

as when someone taps a maple in spring

and I could see it thrumming in your chest

desiring like sweetness to run free.


She spoke him the words with her eyes, his wound

visible on her face.  And with her hands

she drilled a small hole in his heart, tiniest

of openings for the world to slip in.

## Feeding the Dog So He Can Die

I am reading his breath.
I am traveling through his bright lungs,
my open hand a grassy knoll,
a mound of earth held out to him,
the scrap of meat bait in a trap.
Not that November is anything
other than death, which is why I like
its stamped leaves on my forehead
or to see them floated like children's toys
on Thursday's snow as if
*whispering only, please*
had fallen from the sky.
Language on the skin is dangerous.
Even funny webbed prints
on white seas of grass
come perilously close
to song. May I never see
a fox dragging a bloody stump
through winter's scrubbed forest.
Or a purple slur circling the edge
of a frozen pond. Or to know
which part was salt,
which part bone,
when ice closed,
crystal by crystal,
his unquiet eye.
My dog neither craves
nor wants. He is the shadow

of a shadow
that follows a child
home. If you do not believe
this gentle cloud exists,
turn to the last stillness.
Why wander elsewhere?

## Good Dog, Die

I.

Who dragged the chair through soggy grassland
then waited on birds, as if their survival

depended upon a scattering of cracked seeds?
Whose body, with its back to the sun,

watched the tide recede,
wind climbing the mind's rickety staircase?

It could have been either one of us
walking the marsh's mute audience of reeds.

II.

One held the dog's head between his palms.
The other whispered in his ear: *good dog, die.*

The other's eyes shut against what she remembered
of his face, the music of early snowfall

on his fur.  Mercy has little to do
with death, very little.  Nothing could be stranger.

But then we dug the hole, chose the stone
before the needle stung his skin.

Then someone tapped us awake.
(It was many years later;

it was later the same day.)
*Look, a boat is floating down the street.*

Nothing could have been stranger,
yet there it was—

dog, boat, the tide running out.

## Deer at Dusk

Patches of trampled grass, in the field,
in the orchard.  Dusk like thick water, folds of gray.

Their necks rippled when they heard my step,
but already twigs had snapped,

and their sprung limbs went soundlessly into the forest,
the late sun glancing off their thighs. They were bright coins

stopped in the day's decline,
then they were gone.

Even in early light, winter brushed their sides.
*What's coming will come soon enough*, I thought,

and then the old sadness lifted. In the poet's garden,
blue bells lining the path from his garden gate to his door,

he and I talked of loneliness and children and why there is joy
in living a life from which something is missing.

Looking in the wrong direction,
I watched the waves roll in.

Deer emptied the meadow.
A moth circled with her green moon.

## In the Mineral Dark

In the cold petals of sleep,
without fear or trepidation,
angels fly. Fastened to whiteness,
fugitive stars guide them
to my empty meadows.

They brush my eyes
with their heated bodies
and forests rise from stone,
the radiant flux of history
written in flecks and swirls.

They trace the mineral dark
with their soft wings
and leaf by leaf trees root
in the freshet of the night.
Blackbird by blackbird,

branches feather
the unfurnished dream.
A small stream rises,
ample, impossibly clear.

## The Quiet

No one time can claim its hollow center.

I fall into it and risk
my name and history.

All is equal in the new air:
The open book unraveling

its tale that *will* end,
the nest of cedar waxwings

knitted to a broad branch,
the wind knocking the yellow leaves.

*Time will tell* is not true.
The birch trees weaken;

this is their future.
The quiet passes between their weighted boughs.

When I shut my eyes
a boat sails to its final destination.

The heroine leans against the rail
and taps her fingers

along its cold edge.
When I lift the book

it has the weight of feathers.
I cannot pick up my life

where it left off.

## Schoodic Peninsula

When the moon hung its nail
at the end of the world
we turned off the lights
and let the stars
replace what we had been saying.
Then a deer (which was once
darkness) stepped
across the road
and became forest
again. If I practice
walking I am footsteps
on the lively fungus.
When I gaze at the white
lichen I am the moon.
When blackberries
print seeds on my lips
I am the sweet season
that houses summer,
fragrant, waiting to close.

## The Path Your Hand Makes

When you left
I stood in the furniture of light
And held your wave,

Dazzled by the contemplation
Of space, your fingers pressed
Against a vacant now,

And it seemed
All the missing and the dead
Had traveled up the river to my feet.

Everything I say
Drives off in the wrong direction
But you.

So many days
Pass through
The snow-stream of my mind.

The stepping stones
That were yours
Are now mine.

## To the Place Without Names

Their bodies floated on the wreckage of love,
they thought it a river to the sea.

She took his hand and placed it on her breast
while her mind formed around ideas

greater than the two of them—
*perfection, suffering.*

Light dwindled to a dot and leaves fled.
Words like *reckless* and *new* were never retrieved.

They glided over boulders and fallen trees.
Grief carried them to the juncture of wind and stream.

Salt sharpened the air, a brief repose.
The shoreline glistened, then passed.

## Like That or Not at All

It was evening. Blackbirds and mice
were landing on rooftops.
I searched my pockets for what was missing.
A neon sign spelled *om. Home? Omen?*
Neither direction was like stepping off
into daybreak. I looked behind me for a noise
that had rustled the leaves, but only hedges
framed the darkness. My hands discovered that sleep
is not only for the shoes under my bed.
If you had flown past on gaudy wings
I would have mimed: *tulip, heirloom.*
When it was happening, we were wading
through seeds. I had to clear a space
for the pages of "The Last Known Tricks
of St. Verisimiltude," the one with no arms
who kept pulling memory from her sleeveless kimono.
When it was happening, I found the last poet.
He was tending bluebells, he was swatting mosquitoes,
he was remembering the old place
that had propelled him toward happiness. He said,
"When it happens, let the birds write on the sky."
"When it happens, all miracles look like empty boxes."
"When it happens, you will not know which words
to abandon." Faithful to appearances,
he snapped off dead blossoms
and dropped them in a bucket.

*for Stanley Kunitz*

## I'll Build You a House

... all I want is a human window
in a house whose roof is my life.
                    —Ilya Kaminsky

Here's the orchard, here's the leaf.

Here's the beveled slant of dusk.

Here's the jamb to hang the door.

Here's the flame that heats the stone.

Here's the rasp that smoothes the pine.

Here's the rusty path, the crumbs,

the rot that silts the runnel's pull.

Here's the window, here's the eye

the raven cast. Here's the granite,

here's the latch.  Here's the open

book, the light. Here's the fruit,

the bone, the seed. I'll raise

the house that rides the earth.

I'll gather plums, I'll plant my touch.

*for Steve*

## A Late Proposal

end over end
each piece
fitting into the next
all morning we worked I forgot
what I had been thinking
what had kept me
where nothing lives
well or easily
let's live by a river
he said looking up at me
then the last plank
slipped into place
and then he asked me
would I yes

## My Friend Brings Me a Cedar Waxwing to Release into the Orchard

Inside the white box
the bird bats her body
against the cardboard sides.

*This is how you still her.*
My friend cups her hands
around imaginary softness.
*Like this,* she says,
and lifts her closed palms.
I do not know the name for this gesture.
I do know its formal desire
hinges on the music of the wrist.

It is almost spring.
We sit in that brief time,
when afternoon leans against the light.
Rain turns to snow and back again.
Thick black buds are shining.

The bird's wings flap.
I measure her fierceness
against the room's silence.

My sweetheart is hiking in snow;
I think it is the only language
he knows: white breath
on the skin.  I write love letters
with my finger on the sky.

Inside the white box
the bird dreams an eye,
then a beak, then a wing.
Word by word
she sets herself free.

*for Betsy*

*Acknowledgments & Notes*

## Acknowledgments:

*Ars Interpres:* "November's White Apples," "The Bells of Autumn," "To the Place Without Names"

*Crab Creek Review:* "Indigo Bunting"

*Friends of Acadia Journal:* "In the Mineral Dark," "The Path Your Hand Makes," "Schoodic Peninsula"

*Hawk and Handsaw:* "Shattered Branches" (forthcoming)

*Hanging Loose:* "Minus Zero" (as "In the Zero Hours")

*Harvard Review:* *"HAARESCHNEIDERAUM: The Haircutting Room"*

*In Posse Review* (on line): "Pleasures of the Natural World"

*Kestrel*: "An Apology for Silence," "The Moon Is White"

*New Millennium Writings:* "My Friend Brings Me a Cedar Waxwing To Release into the Orchard" (finalist in 2006 contest). The poem will also appear in the 2009 Women Artists Datebook, Syracuse Cultural Workers.

*Poetry:* "A Simple Love Story," "The Quiet"

*Rivendell,* "Snow In Autumn"

*The Worcester Review:* "Deer at Dusk"

*West Branch:* "She Watches a House Burn As If It Were Her Own"

*What Is Home:* the Portsmouth Poet Laureate Program, "I'll Build You a House"

*Women Artists Datebook, Syracuse Cultural Workers:* "My Mother's Bureau"

The following poems appeared in *The Singed Horizon*, Philbrick Award winning chapbook, Providence Athenaeum: "She Watches a House Burn As If It Were Her Own," "Still Life Minus You," "Blue," "The Moon Is White," "The Singed Horizon"

Thanks to Ranger Kate Petrie and the Acadia National Park Artist-in-Residence Program, especially to Ranger Kate for her support and friendship during three residencies on Schoodic Peninsula where several of these poems were written. Also, I wish to thank the NH State Council on the Arts for their generous Artist Opportunity Grant that provided travel funds for my time on Schoodic Peninsula.

I am also grateful to the Philbrick family and the Providence Athenaeum for publishing my chapbook, *The Singed Horizon*. I am eternally grateful to Robert Creeley for selecting my work for publication.

For providing me with a public forum and an opportunity to create a community wide poetry project, I wish to thank the Portsmouth Poet Laureate Program.

To those who have sustained me and encouraged my efforts over the years I offer my deepest gratitude. A very special thank you to the poets at Skimmilk Farm and Hildred Crill, Mary Fister, Elizabeth Kirschner, Grace Mattern, Candice Stover, and Katherine Towler for reading these poems in progress.

Lastly, I wish to thank my husband, Stephen White, for never wavering in his belief in me. His faith is in every poem.

Notes:

*HAARESCHNEIDERAUM: The Haircutting Room;* several details come from *Evidence of Evil* by Timothy W. Wryneck, The New Yorker, November 15, 1993

The first lines of *She Watches A House Burn As if It Were Her Own* are borrowed from Sherod Santos' Contributor's Notes and comments, *The Best American Poetry 1991.*

---

On the Cover: *Grape Leaves with Lesser Goldfinch Nest,* a photograph by Sharon Beals. More of her work can be found at www.sharonbeals.com.

A book of Sharon Beals photography of bird nests will be published in the near future, something to look forward to.